D0119086

YUKON

COLOUR OF THE LAND – PHOTOGRAPHY BY RICHARD HARTMIER

YUKON

COLOUR OF THE LAND – PHOTOGRAPHY BY RICHARD HARTMIER

LOST MOOSE

THE YUKON PUBLISHERS

WHITEHORSE 1995

Published by Lost Moose, the Yukon Publishers
For information on other books "from the north about the north,"
write, fax or telephone:

58 Kluane Crescent, Whitehorse, Yukon Canada Y1A 3G7
Fax 403-668-6223. Phone 403-668-3441, 403-668-5076.

Canadian Cataloguing in Publication Data

Hartmier, Richard, 1951–

　　　Yukon : colour of the land

　　ISBN 0-9694612-7-5

　　　1. Yukon Territory--Pictorial works. I. Title.
FC4012.H37 1995　971.9'103'0222　　C95-910262-0
F1091.H37 1995

To my mother and father, who wanted me to get a real job.
　　　　　　　　　　　　　　　　— Richard Hartmier

Design by Mike Rice/Catalyst Communications

Printed in Canada by Friesen Printers, Altona, Manitoba

INTRODUCTION

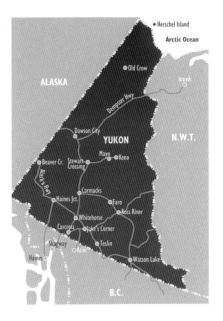

The Yukon is a place to travel endless ribbons of wilderness highway, explore the history of the Klondike Gold Rush or head into the plentiful backcountry.

Irrepressible images are etched into the memories of those who experience this remarkable land. It's the colour of the land, painted by a special kind of light in the north, that creates these vivid impressions.

The colour of the land changes with the hours, days and weeks of the northern summer. It's found in the plants and animals of this majestic and pristine northern wilderness. It's found along mighty rivers, in mountain passes and in hillside meadows lit brilliantly by flowers under a warm summer sun.

Yukon — Colour of the Land is an invitation to share our home as we see it, and as others will remember it. Come and enjoy.

ALASKA HIGHWAY NEAR JAKE'S CORNER

EMERALD LAKE

FIREWEED, THE YUKON'S FLORAL EMBLEM

GRIZZLY BEAR

ROBERT SERVICE CABIN, DAWSON CITY

Stories

HUNKER CREEK

ALASKA HIGHWAY MILE 1118

CANADA DAY

9

RAFTING THE YUKON RIVER

Dreams

PILOT'S BUTTE, DEMPSTER HIGHWAY

NEAR ROSS RIVER

OTTER FALLS

STERNWHEELER GRAVEYARD NEAR DAWSON   BURWASH LANDING   TUTSHI REMAINS AT CARCROSS

S.S. TUTSHI BEFORE FIRE BURNED IT DOWN

WHITE PASS AND YUKON ROUTE

OLD MINE SITE ON MONTANA MOUNTAIN

SALMON FISHWHEEL NEAR DAWSON   FISH CAMP – A YUKON TRADITION   FISH DRYING NEAR OLD CROW

MIGRATING SALMON AT WHITEHORSE FISH LADDER

TLINGIT DANCE

Tradition

LITTLE ATLIN LAKE

BARRENGROUND CARIBOU CROSSING DEMPSTER HIGHWAY

HUNTING CARIBOU NEAR OLD CROW

NORTHERN LIGHTS AT A WILDERNESS LODGE

SECOND AND MAIN, WHITEHORSE

THE YUKON'S CAPITAL, WHITEHORSE, FROM GREY MOUNTAIN

PTARMIGAN   FEMALE NORTHERN FLICKER   MALLARD

BABY GREAT HORNED OWLS

BABY RAVENS

YOUNG FOX   COAL BLACK GROUND SQUIRREL   PORCUPINE

TUNDRA ON THE DEMPSTER, NEAR THE ARCTIC CIRCLE

Colours

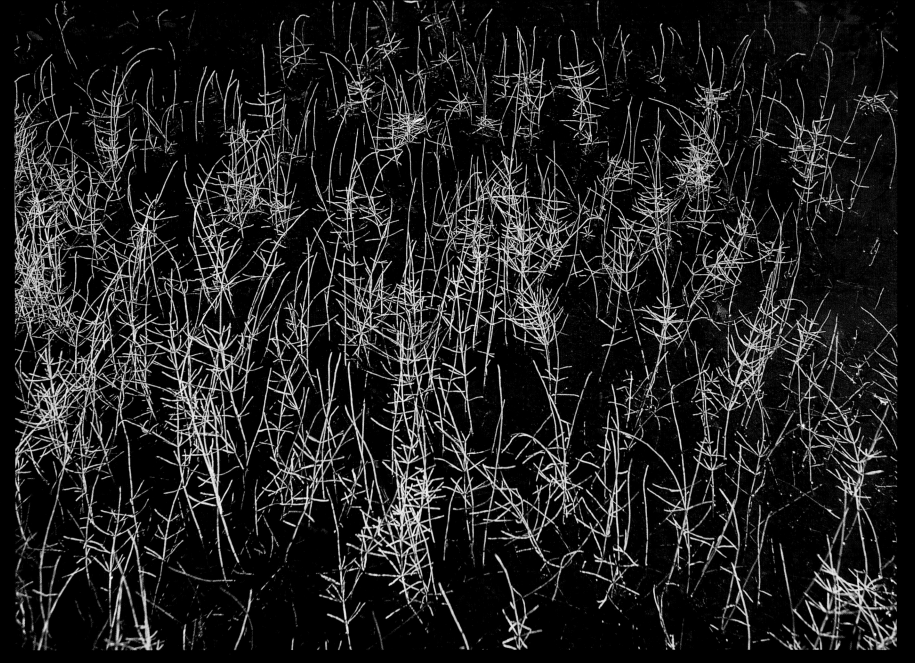

MACLEAN LAKE

NEW GROWTH EMERGES AFTER A FOREST FIRE ON EAGLE PLAINS

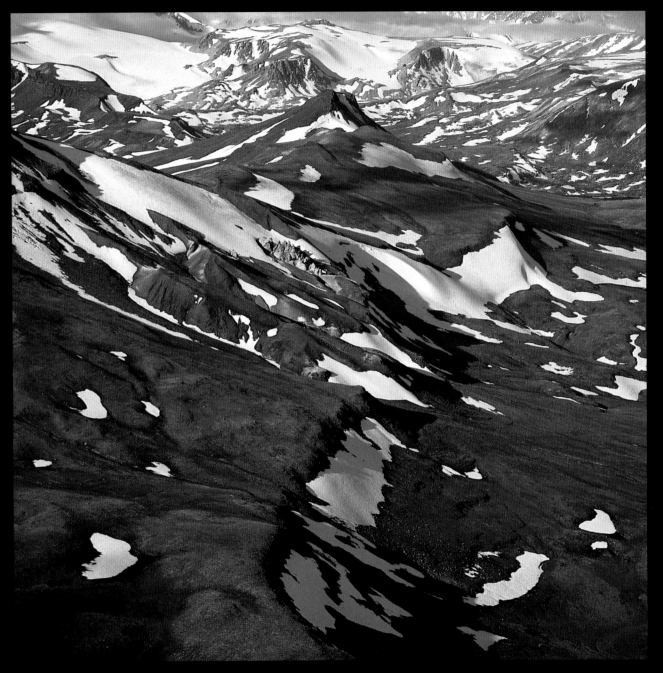

KLUANE PARK

Natural forces

ST. ELIAS RANGE

DONJEK GLACIER   KASKAWULSH GLACIER

DEMPSTER HIGHWAY

STONE HOUSE, MONTANA MOUNTAIN

SPRING, MILES CANYON

51

ON KENO HILL

MIDNIGHT DOME, DAWSON CITY

ROAD RELAY RACE, NEAR WHITEHORSE

NEAR DAWSON

A *place to enjoy*

CYCLIST TRAVELLING THE ALASKA HIGHWAY

COMMISSIONER'S TEA, DAWSON

LAKE LABERGE

ELK   DALL SHEEP   WOODLAND CARIBOU

MOOSE AND CALF

FLOUR PACKING CONTEST AT SOURDOUGH RENDEZVOUS

64 *Winter life*

YUKON QUEST START, WHITEHORSE

SPECIAL CARE FOR DOGS ALONG THE QUEST TRAIL

HEADING INTO DAWSON

PUPPIES AT HOME

Northern sights

WOLF IN THE WILD

ICE CRYSTALS IN UNDERGROUND MINE SHAFT AT GOLD RUN CREEK

40 BELOW IN DAWSON CITY

Winter lights

DAWSON

YOUNG EAGLES IN DIALOGUE

SNOWBIRDS AT HERSCHEL ISLAND

76 *Time passing*

MOOSEHIDE

FORTY MILE

TWELVE MILE

OLD MINE SHAFT UNCOVERED ON HUNKER CREEK

Mining

TOOLS LEFT BEHIND IN AN OLD MINE SHAFT, GOLD RUN CREEK

MINING EQUIPMENT WAITS FOR SPRING

OLD KEYSTONE DRILL, KLONDIKE GOLDFIELDS

83

CABINS OF THE KLONDIKE GOLD RUSH

ABANDONED W.W. II VEHICLE, HAINES ROAD

TARAHNE AT ATLIN

OLD BRIDGE PILINGS, CARCROSS

88

REMAINS OF BRIDGE ON THE SLIMS RIVER

89

TOP OF THE WORLD HIGHWAY

Farther north

DEMPSTER HIGHWAY

HERSCHEL ISLAND IN JULY, I A.M.

ANGLICAN MISSION HOUSE, HERSCHEL ISLAND

95

Scenes remembered

SUNRISE IN MAYO

YUKON HILLS

CARIBOU ENSHROUDED BY FOG ON THE NORTH COAST

S.S. KLONDIKE, WHITEHORSE AT 40 BELOW

GRAVE OF THE LOST PATROL, FORT McPHERSON

At rest

A YUKON ORDER OF PIONEERS GRAVE AT GOLD RUN CREEK

GRAVEYARD AT FORT SELKIRK

CARCROSS

DAWSON CITY, WHERE THE KLONDIKE RIVER FLOWS INTO THE YUKON

DISCOVERY DAY PARADE, DAWSON

SUMMER FUN

DAWSON CITY

DREDGE AT HUNKER CREEK

The Yukon

HART RIVER CAMP

DEER

SUNSET THROUGH FOREST FIRE HAZE

TOMBSTONE MOUNTAINS

OGILVIE MOUNTAINS

FORT SELKIRK